Colin Baxter's
EDINBURGH

First published in Great Britain in 1986 by
Colin Baxter Photography
Lamington, Biggar, Lanarkshire, ML12 6HW
Copyright © Colin Baxter, 1986
All rights reserved

British Library Cataloguing in Publication Data
Baxter, Colin
    Colin Baxter's Edinburgh
    1. Edinburgh (Lothian)—Description—Views
    I. Title
    941.3'40858'0222   DA890.E3
    ISBN 0-948661-01-1

Design Charles Miller Graphics, Edinburgh
Editing and Research Alan Edwards, Edinburgh

Typeset by Hewer Text Composition Services, Edinburgh
Printed by Frank Peters Printers Ltd., Kendal, Cumbria
Bound by Hunter & Foulis Ltd., Edinburgh

Colin Baxter's
EDINBURGH

PHOTOGRAPHS OF THE CAPITAL CITY

COLIN BAXTER PHOTOGRAPHY
LAMINGTON

CONTENTS

BIOGRAPHICAL NOTE

Colin Baxter was born in 1954. He studied photography in Edinburgh from 1978–81, and now lives in rural Lanarkshire. He first gained attention through exhibitions of his work and by publishing a range of postcards, mainly of Scotland. Since then he has brought out collections of cards covering Edinburgh, Glasgow, Bath, Yorkshire, and the Lake District. His first book, 'Scotland – The Light and the Land', a collection of landscapes, was published in 1985.

DUSK OVER THE CITY

ST. GILES' AND SPIRES

INTRODUCTION

SPACE AND SPLENDOUR

My first impression of Scotland's capital, shared by so many visitors emerging from Waverley Station, was of the sheer spaciousness and splendour of the city centre. I don't believe there is another city in Britain that can boast such an eye-catching 'arena' at its centre. The best of Edinburgh is right there in front of you, within the rectangle formed by George Street to the north, the High Street to the south, and Lothian Road and North Bridge to the west and east; with the Castle as centre-piece standing high above Princes Street Gardens. A glance around this magnificent amphitheatre immediately introduces the spectator to the two distinct aspects of the city's character; the Old and New Towns — the cluttered tenements of the sixteenth and seventeenth centuries stacked precariously along the Castle ridge, and, in sharp contrast, the elegant and expansive architecture of the Georgian New Town, clearly a product of the eighteenth century — Edinburgh's Golden Age.

I spent my first years here at college in Marchmont and during that period, as I became more familiar with the city, I saw that it possessed many other facets than those concentrated in the centre. Marchmont itself, while principally a residential area, still had many of the characteristics of smaller self-contained communities, and a visible life of its own. Were it not for the garish advertising in its window, the chemist's, with its array of old apothecaries jars, might have been from another time. In fact until the middle of the eighteenth century this area was cut off from the main town by the South Loch which was drained and subsequently became 'The Meadows' – a beautiful tree-lined grassy expanse and a notable feature of the south side of the city. Doubtless Edinburgh's varied terrain of volcanic rock, small lochs, and steep wooded valleys played its part in ensuring that the various 'village' communities on the outskirts of the town retained their own characteristics – even as the city itself gradually encompassed them. The inquisitive visitor can still find many such places tucked away in odd corners; some of them like Stockbridge, the Dean Village, or the Colonies, only a short walk from Princes Street.

During my time at college I was not immediately drawn to the possibilities of photographing the city itself. Perhaps because I was allowed, and encouraged, to experiment creatively I tended to use photography in a more abstract way. I was taking photographs in Edinburgh certainly, but in such a way that they could have been anywhere. In my final year I was concentrating on landscape photography, partly because I was living outside Edinburgh but also because I had become aware of the enormous potential for landscape work in the north and west of Scotland – and, of course, because I love to be in the Highlands. Even so, I was starting to take a few pictures within the city which were based on a different approach from my earlier 'abstract' work and which were recognisably of Edinburgh – a window or a detail of a New Town facade perhaps. Gradually too, I was becoming interested in photographing 'townscapes' as a natural extension of my landscape work, and discovering, in the process, that Edinburgh was an excellent subject for this type of photography. Like Rome, Edinburgh is built upon seven hills and, among the various vantage points, Salisbury Crags, Arthur's Seat, and Calton Hill all offer splendid views of the city. It is a pity that there isn't a hill similar to Arthur's Seat in the west of the city, but that is perhaps too much to ask! Inadvertently I have come to agree with Sir Walter Scott who once said, 'If I were to choose a spot from which the rising or setting sun could be seen to greatest advantage, it would be that wild path of semicircular rocks, called Salisbury Crags'.

From whatever point one chooses one is faced with a vista peppered with spires, domes, and towers of every description, with the castle looming large at its centre and the whole image enlivened by the changing contours of the land as it stretches northwards from the Braid Hills to the shining arm of the Firth of Forth. It is a feature of this view that it contains virtually no high-rise blocks and, ignoring the occasional architectural blunder — such as the tower erected by the University in George Square, the modernisation of sections of Princes Street, or the government offices behind the Castle, Edinburgh, seen from a distance, is strikingly beautiful. As the smoke rises above the Old Town on an autumn evening 'Auld Reekie' appears before you, looking much as it did when the name was first coined; and looking out across the New Town on a clear summer's day one can easily see how Scotland's capital came to be known as 'The Athens of the North'. Even towns like Bath or York, both famous for their well-preserved architecture, lack the range and spaciousness of Edinburgh.

By comparison Glasgow's skyline is a shambles of high-rises and a photographer has to work quite hard to find views of that city which capture any feeling of the past. In fact when I am photographing Glasgow I tend to look for the more ordinary things — a stained glass window, an unusual piece of masonry, street lamps, shop fronts, and so on. These are the things which make Glasgow interesting and atmospheric in its own right, but no-one familiar with Scotland's two main cities can fail to be struck by the contrasts they present, despite being only fifty miles apart. Appropriately perhaps, my range of Glasgow postcards contains one of a motorway; an association I would be unlikely to make with Edinburgh.

I am often asked why there are no people in my photographs and I suppose the reason is that my first concern in photography is with 'composition'. People can easily distract the eye – by the colour of their clothing or the way that they are caught at the crucial moment – and this tends, unintentionally, to make them the focus of attention. In another way they effectively 'date' an image, and this is something I try to avoid. My style is essentially different from the old approach to 'postcard' photography in which it is unusual to find images of towns or villages which do not include people. In a way I am trying to bring a purer, less complicated image to the fore. Nevertheless I like to think that my work does contain a human element, as in the photograph of the bicycle in James' Court.

Again, I don't see myself as 'documenting' city life in the way that previous generations of photographers did, particularly in the early days and between the wars, my concerns being mainly with form and composition. In the photograph of Victoria Street for example I have deliberately cut it off above the level of the cars and pedestrians because they would distract from the basic idea; the composition of various levels of buildings.

Inevitably of course some of the photographs have already become documents of Edinburgh's past. I recently tried to revisit Tweeddale Court on the Royal Mile only to find it boarded up and extensive renovations taking place. The original photograph is one of the few I have taken which shows the darker side of the city, hinting, as it does, at the fact that during the nineteenth century much of the Old Town was little more than a slum; the wealthy and well-to-do citizens having by then migrated to the New Town. Since then, and particularly over the last ten years, a great deal of restoration and conservation work has been carried out in both the Old and New Towns, particularly around the Lawnmarket, the Grassmarket, and the lower parts of

JAMES' COURT

the New Town, and this has contributed greatly to the impression of Edinburgh as a city largely unspoilt by the vagaries of modern town planning. Obviously there is still a fair amount to be done — take for example the 'gap site' in the middle of the High Street which has been empty for decades — but even as it stands Edinburgh is full of the resonances of a rich and varied past. In this book I have tried to capture some of these resonances, not, as I have said, in order to document the city, but in an attempt to build up a series of impressions which convey its atmosphere. One thing which continues to surprise me however, is the fact that the Royal Mile, unlike similar streets in other European cities, has not been pedestrianised. Surely there would be no better way to explore the heart of the city than walking the mile from the Castle to Holyrood Palace, with the historic buildings cleaned and restored and a few flowerboxes in the windows, unimpeded by city-centre traffic.

The earliest photographs in this book were among those taken for my first range of 'Just Edinburgh' cards which came out in 1984. Many of these cards have been included here although obviously there is a difference between selecting postcards and compiling a book. With cards it is not always easy to know in advance what will prove popular and, despite personal preferences and objective opinions, I have at times been proved wrong with my selections. There is no better way of getting critical feedback on your work than marketing post-cards; but this is not to say that all my work is geared in that direction. I have taken many photographs which do not have a commercial value as cards but which I nevertheless regard as being successful in other contexts — as prints perhaps, or as an integral part of a book. In book form I feel I have the chance to present some of these and to give a broader view of my work, which can be both more personal and more adventurous.

When I am actually working I must say that I get as much satisfaction from a photograph that was easy to take as I do from one that was technically more difficult.

RAMSAY GARDEN · CASTLE HILL

Technical considerations are really a secondary matter in photography and no amount of wizardry can make a good photograph out of inadequate subject matter or poor composition. My picture of Ramsay Garden illustrates what I mean by 'composition'. It required very little technical expertise – in fact it's almost a 'snap' – but it works. It amazes me that no-one else has published this particular photograph. All you need to do is stand on the bank in front of the building, preferably with some late afternoon sun to accentuate the shadows, and you have a ready-made composition, full of interesting detail, which fits perfectly into a 35mm viewfinder. I also get a lot of pleasure from actually 'seeing' a certain composition which is not immediately obvious and sometimes, in retrospect, I wonder how I ever managed to achieve some of them. One such photograph was taken looking across the Royal Scottish Academy to the Old Town from a roundabout on George Street. I don't know how many times I must have driven round there before I 'saw' that view. In that instance I used a telephoto lens, which is an ideal tool for fashioning slightly unusual views. In certain places, Waverley Market for example, it is almost a challenge to find strong images and pick them out from the confusion.

As I generally work outside, natural light plays an important part in my approach and although I tend to work instinctively I do go to some places under certain conditions in order to achieve an effect. The cover photograph was taken from Salisbury Crags on a crisp January afternoon with a warm, oblique, almost summerish light slanting onto the covering of snow – a wonderful time to be there. I have always been interested in unusual or dramatic light conditions and the fact that these can change so rapidly, particularly in Scotland's unpredictable climate, really forces me to work spontaneously. I like to wander about, with the minimum of planning, and I find that most of my successful photographs are taken in this way. In general terms one learns which sort of conditions are suitable

THE OLD TOWN FROM THE NEW TOWN

for certain subjects — the photographs of the pubs are mostly taken in the fine balance of light between daylight and twilight for example — but a city like Edinburgh is full of surprises which help to keep the process fresh and exciting. A recent discovery was the entrance to Panmure Close in the Canongate with its wrought iron gate decorated with two red flowers. Hundreds of people must walk past that gate every day. I wonder how many of them notice its existence. The history of that particular close is recorded on several plaques on the gate and this combination of historical and visual interest is something else I try to achieve when possible.

Contrary to popular belief I don't use filters when taking my photographs. Each year, when I am exhibiting and selling prints and cards in the Old Assembly Close during the Festival, I am amused to overhear comments to the effect that certain photographs were taken with a filter. This is not the case, although by handprinting my own work I have control over brightness and colour and this enables me to recreate some of the visual subtlety which can be lost in a 'straight' machine print.

This book is not intended to be a definitive photographic record of Edinburgh, nor could it be. Mostly I have concentrated my attention on that central arena which seems to me to express the very essence of this great city, and I know that within this area alone there is still a wealth of undiscovered material. I first became interested in photography because I saw that there were no limits to what it could express, and I will continue to photograph Edinburgh because it too is limitless in its beauty and character.

Colin Baxter

VICTORIA STREET

Even in the 1840s efforts were being made to ensure that changes to the Old Town were in keeping with what already existed. Victoria Street, built at this time, necessitated the destruction of several closes, alleys, and wynds around the Lawnmarket.

THE CASTLE FROM BRUNTSFIELD

From practically every viewpoint the Castle emerges; dominating the
landscape of the city and lending it a note of grandeur.

THE MEADOWS IN SPRING

'There has never in my time been any single place in or near Edinburgh, which has so distinctly been the resort at once of our philosophy and our fashion. Under these trees walked, and talked, and meditated, all our literary and scientific, and many of our legal worthies.'

Lord Cockburn recalling the Meadows, about 1820

THE KENILWORTH · ROSE STREET   THE CAFE ROYAL · WEST REGISTER STREET

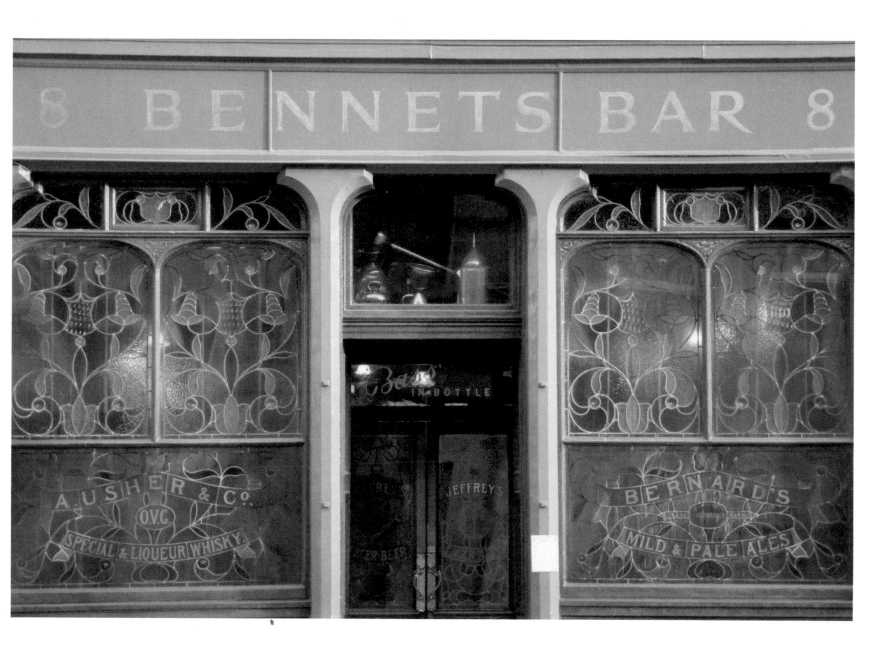

BENNET'S BAR · LEVEN STREET

Stained glass windows are a feature of many of Edinburgh's older public houses, the interiors of which have often been preserved from Victorian and Edwardian times. These pubs are particularly fine examples. As recently as 1969 the Cafe Royal, with its tiled murals, marble floor and huge Circle Bar, was saved from demolition.

'If I were to choose a spot from which the rising or setting sun could be seen to greatest possible advantage, it would be that wild path winding around the foot of the high belt of semicircular rocks, called Salisbury Crags, and marking the verge of the steep descent which slopes down into the glen on the south-eastern side of the city of Edinburgh. . . . When a piece of scenery so beautiful, yet so varied, – so exciting by its intricacy, and yet so sublime, – is lighted up by the tints of morning or of evening, the effect approaches near to enchantment.'

from 'The Heart of Midlothian' by Sir Walter Scott 1818

THE CITY FROM SALISBURY CRAGS

THE NORTH BRITISH HOTEL

Old photographs of the city show a more modest building occupied by
Cranston and Elliot 'House Furnishers, Costumiers and Silk Mercers' on
the site now occupied by the North British Hotel. When the hotel was built
in 1902 it was described as 'coarse and obstructive' by critics of its rather
overbearing style; but like the Scott Monument, a Gothic fantasy which
had faced similar charges forty years previously, it has come to be accepted
as a natural feature of the city centre.

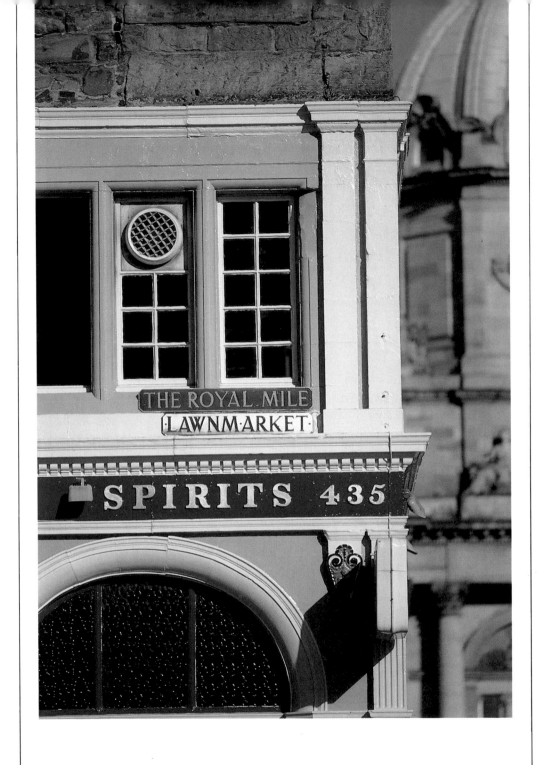

DEACON BRODIE'S TAVERN · LAWNMARKET

Deacon Brodie's stands at the corner of Bank Street and the Lawnmarket,
an enduring reminder of one of Edinburgh's most infamous citizens – a
respected town councillor by day, and a burglar by night.

THE MOUND AND NORTH BRIDGE

'Whereas the Bridge building over the North Loch of this City (whereby an early and commodious communication will be made between the city and the fields on the north) is already considerably advanced, the Magistrates and Town-Council are now taking the necessary measures for the further improvement of the city, by feuing out the said fields for the purpose of building houses thereon . . .'

Extract from an advertisement inviting architects to present plans for the New Town

WAVERLEY MARKET

Little trace remains of the Old Waverley Market, once a centre for
exhibitions, flower shows, and carnivals, at the east end of Princes Street.
Its new counterpart combines ambitious design with an emphasis on
small shops and stalls which market a bewildering array of products,
many of them traditionally Scottish.

PRINCES STREET GARDENS

These gardens are the focal point of the city centre. In the fourteenth
century they were known as the King's Garden and were used as a
tournament ground. In 1460 the Nor' Loch was formed here by damming
a burn, creating an added defence for the Castle. The loch was drained
in the early part of the nineteenth century and the gardens opened to
the public in 1850. Even on a misty winter's day, with the trees bare,
they have a charm of their own.

PANMURE CLOSE · CANONGATE

One of the plaques on the gate reads: 'Here the Jacobite Earl of
Panmure had his town house, later occupied by Adam Smith,
author of The Wealth of Nations'.

WARDROP'S COURT · LAWNMARKET

Four dragons guard the entrance to this court, built in 1790 by
John Wardrop – a burgess of the city.

WHITEHORSE CLOSE · CANONGATE

Originally the Royal Mews, and later an inn and coach-house, a visitor
in 1754 could have read the following handbill posted outside: 'All that
are desirous to pass from Edinburgh to London or any other place on
their road, let them repair to the White Horse Cellar in Edinburgh at
which place they may be received in a Stage Coach every Monday and
Friday which performs the whole journey in eight days (if God permits)
and sets forth at five in the morning'.

DRAGON IN RAMSAY GARDEN

THE OLD TOWN FROM THE NEW TOWN

A statue of Queen Victoria and four massive sphinxes stand on top of
the Royal Scottish Academy. Beyond them even the tenements of the
Old Town are dwarfed by the city's highest steeple, that of the
Highland Church of Tolbooth St. Johns, on Castle Hill. Here we
see the contrast between the grandness of Georgian design and the
picturesque romance of the older style.

THE CASTLE FROM THE GRASSMARKET

ANCHOR CLOSE · HIGH STREET

'Beside the door sat the landlady, a large, fat woman, in a towering
head-dress and large-flowered silk gown, who bowed to everyone passing.
The house was noted for its suppers of tripe, rizzared haddocks, mince
collops, and hashes, which never cost more than sixpence a head.'

description of Dawney Douglas's Tavern in Anchor Close, about 1790

**THE ROYAL MUSEUM OF SCOTLAND
CHAMBERS STREET**

The main hall of the Museum is a striking example of Victorian design at
its best. Appropriately, the engineering and scientific sections of the
collection pay homage to the many Scots-born pioneers of the Industrial
Revolution, and, as a feat of engineering, the building itself is a living
embodiment of that era.

THE NATIONAL GALLERY AND
THE CALEDONIAN HOTEL

Looking west, the imposing facade of William Playfair's National Gallery
is softened by the red sandstone of the Caledonian Hotel in the distance.
The hotel was built at the turn of the century, next to what was then the
Caledonian Railway Station. The spires of the various West End churches
add the finishing touch to a typical Edinburgh skyline.

MELVILLE STREET · WEST END

'I charge you not to think of settling in London till you have first seen our
New Town which exceeds anything you have seen in any part of the world.'

David Hume 1771

THE CITY FROM ARTHUR'S SEAT

NORTH BRIDGE AND CALTON HILL

The original North Bridge was completed in 1772. It was the beginning of
a thoroughfare stretching southwards beyond the old Flodden Wall to
Nicolson Park. Before its rebuilding in 1897, Robert Louis Stevenson
recalled how he would lean over the 'great bridge' to 'watch the trains
smoking out and vanishing into the tunnel on a voyage to brighter skies'.

THE COWGATE

The Cowgate, an extension of Holyrood Road leading from the Palace to
the Grassmarket, was originally a country lane along which cattle were
taken to pasture. In the fifteenth century it became a fashionable suburb
for the gentry but gradually degenerated until, in 1865, a visitor to the
city could remark that the inhabitants were 'morally and geographically
the lower orders'. Two arches pass over what is now a rather sombre
street – George IV Bridge and South Bridge.

SHOPS · ST. MARY'S STREET

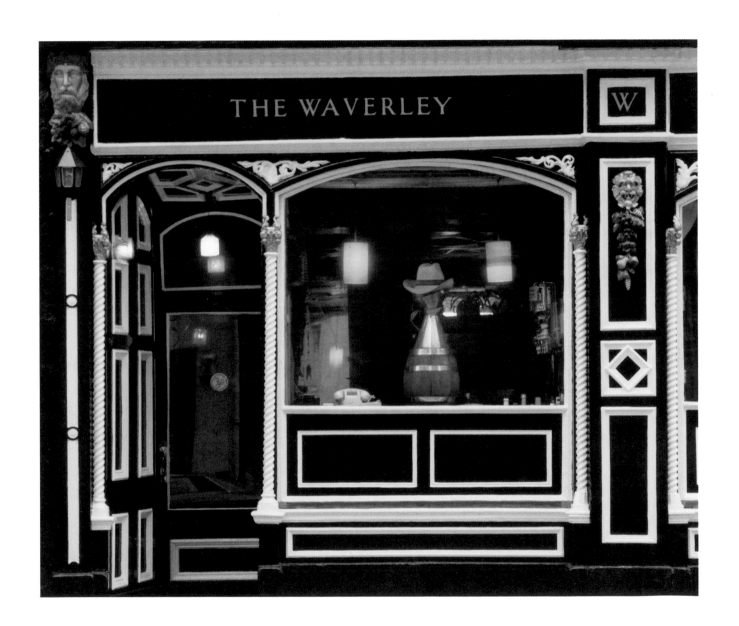

THE WAVERLEY BAR · ST. MARY'S STREET

THE ROYAL SCOTTISH ACADEMY WITH FIFE
IN THE DISTANCE

Looking out across the Firth of Forth to the ancient Kingdom of Fife,
where the name 'Auld Reekie' is thought to have originated. An onlooker
from that shore would have seen the smoke hovering over the city, in Sir
Walter Scott's phrase, 'as the goss-hawk hangs over a plump of young wild ducks'.

THE NATIONAL GALLERY OF SCOTLAND AND THE ROYAL SCOTTISH ACADEMY

The National Gallery and the R.S.A. stand at the foot of the Mound. The Mound is the central link between the Old and New Towns and was constructed using an estimated two million cartloads of earth from the New Town excavations. Both these buildings were the work of William Playfair, the capital's most prolific architect; the National Gallery being completed in 1857, the year of his death.

THE MILITARY TATTOO AND
THE FESTIVAL FIREWORKS

Two of the most popular events in Edinburgh's annual Festival, the Tattoo
and the fireworks both utilise the magnificent backdrop of the castle at
night. The fireworks display is coordinated with a live performance of
Handel's 'Music For Royal Fireworks' in Princes Street Gardens.

SHOP · WEST NICOLSON STREET

A brightly coloured Georgian-style shopfront in the Southside.

PRINCES STREET

Of all the original New Town, Princes Street has suffered most at the hands
of developers. Two hundred years of haphazard building and rebuilding
have left their mark on what was once considered to be the most beautiful
street in Europe. However, the magnificent open view to the south – of the
Old Town, the Castle, and the Gardens – remains its redeeming feature. In
the original plan George Street was conceived as the main street, and the
whole area was to be strictly residential. Nowadays of course Princes Street
is one of the country's busiest shopping avenues.

THE CITY

'In this one valley there may be seen, shown one above and behind another by the accidents of the ground, buildings of almost every style upon the globe. Egyptian and Greek temples, Venetian palaces and Gothic spires, all huddled one over another in a most admired disorder.'

from 'Edinburgh: Picturesque Notes' by Robert Louis Stevenson 1878

WAVERLEY PENS · BLAIR STREET

What better way to advertise a pen than with the image of that great wordsmith Sir Walter Scott? Still to be seen on the frontage of Waverley Cameron Ltd., makers of 'The Pen of the Empire', is the quaint legend:
'They come as a Boon and a Blessing to men,
The Pickwick, the Owl, and the Waverley Pen.'
(next page)

WAVERLEY

PEN
THE WORLD'S FAVOURITE

BOONS & BLESSINGS

THE
PICKWICK
THE
OWL
THE
WAVERLEY

WAVERLEY FOUNTAIN PEN

They come as a Boon and a Blessing to men
The Pickwick, the Owl, and the Waverley Pen

6^d & 1^s PER BOX
They come as a b
The Pickwick, the

MACNIVEN & CAMERON, LT^D

WAVERLEY

THE WORLD-FAVOURITE
PEN

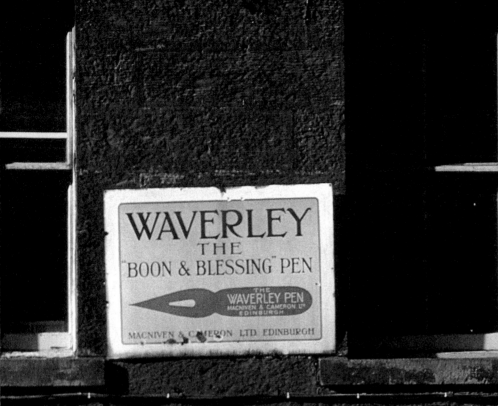

WAVERLEY
THE
"BOON & BLESSING" PEN

THE WAVERLEY PEN
MACNIVEN & CAMERON LTD
EDINBURGH

MACNIVEN & CAMERON LTD EDINBURGH

AT ALL STATIONERS

and a blessing to men
and the Waverley Pen"
EDINBURGH

THE
BOONS & BLESSINGS

THE
OWL
THE PICKWICK   THE WAVERLEY

"They come as a Boon and a Blessing to men
The Pickwick, the Owl, and the Waverley Pen."

WAVERLEY

EDINBURGH CASTLE

Standing 437 feet high on basalt rock created by a volcanic eruption,
the Castle is one of Scotland's most spectacular fortresses. Ice Age
glaciers made its north and south sides almost vertical and it can only
be approached with ease from the east. The name Castle Rock came
into being in the eleventh century when the crude hill fortress was
converted into the royal residence of Malcolm III. St. Margaret's Chapel,
named after Malcolm's Saxon wife, is the oldest building in the Castle and
was probably built by her son David I.

THE CASTLE ESPLANADE

OLD TOWN SKYLINE

TWEEDDALE COURT · HIGH STREET

This photograph gives some indication of the fact that after the building
of the New Town the closes and courts of the Old Town fell into disrepair
and were gradually reduced to slums. It was estimated that in 1850 some
High Street tenements had two hundred and fifty people living in sixty
rooms – with no running water or sanitation.

RAMSAY GARDEN · CASTLE HILL

This spectacular cluster of tall, Georgian-style houses dates from the late
Victorian era. It was built by Sir Patrick Geddes and is a model of
organised town planning, of which it is one of the earliest examples.
The name is derived from the fact that Allan Ramsay, the poet,
had a house here previously.

THE HOME OF THE HAMBURGER
PRINCES STREET

The twin spires of the General Assembly of the Church of Scotland on the Mound are reflected in the windows of the Princes Street Wimpy Bar. The immaculate restoration of the exterior of this building at the junction with Castle Street should serve as a model for future developers.

WAVERLEY MARKET BARROW

One of the many small stalls to be found in the city's newest shopping
centre at the east end of Princes Street.

CHIMNEYPOTS AND THE FIRTH OF FORTH

Edinburgh is, in the words of G. K. Chesterton, 'a sudden city. Great roads
rush down like rivers in spate. Great buildings rush up like rockets'.

'TRIGGER' ON HIS MILK-ROUND

A sight no longer seen in the city – one of the old St. Cuthbert's milk horses
on his morning round. These were the last milk horses to be used in
Britain. Four of the original horses are now used for weddings and
processions. The owners of the splendid collection of old coaches are
coach-painters to the Royal Family.

THE GLASSMARKET · JEFFREY STREET

GEORGE STREET

The foreground statue of William Pitt and the dome of West Register
House in Charlotte Square, as seen from George Street.

ARTHUR'S SEAT

'To the east of the town itself are two mountains, the one called Arthur's
Seat, the other, which faces the north, the Hill of the Wild Boar. The
surrounding country is extremely fertile, with pleasant meadows, little
woods, lakes, streamlets, and more than a hundred castles.'

from an account of Edinburgh by Alexander Alesius 1550

INTERNATIONAL NEWSAGENT · HIGH STREET

Where do you go for a copy of Le Figaro, the Jerusalem Post, or the Wall
Street Journal? The International Newsagent stocks 700 titles.

BRUSHMAKER · VICTORIA STREET

FISHMONGER · ELM ROW

This heraldic panel was originally over the entrance of the gatehouse which stood at the bottom of the Canongate. It bears the Royal Arms for King James V.

THE PALACE OF HOLYROODHOUSE

The Palace of Holyroodhouse stands at the foot of the Royal Mile. It is Scotland's official Royal Residence and has, for over nine hundred years, borne witness to the turbulent history of the capital city. James IV, Mary of Guise, Mary Queen of Scots, Oliver Cromwell, and Bonnie Prince Charlie are among the many figures associated with the Palace.

NOBLE'S BAR · CONSTITUTION STREET

THE GUILDFORD ARMS
WEST REGISTER STREET

CALTON HILL FROM SALISBURY CRAGS

'The east of new Edinburgh is guarded by a craggy hill, of no great
elevation, which the town embraces. You mount by stairs in a cutting
of the rock to find yourself in a field of monuments. Dugald Stewart has
the honours of situation and architecture; Burns is memorialised lower
down upon a spur; Lord Nelson, as befits a sailor, gives his name to the
topgallant of the Calton Hill. But the chief feature is an unfinished range
of columns, 'the Modern Ruin' as it has been called, an imposing object
from far and near. It was meant to be a National Monument; and
its present state is a very suitable monument to certain national
characteristics. The old Observatory – a quaint brown building on the
edge of the steep – and the new Observatory – a classical edifice with a
dome – occupy the central portion of the summit. All these are scattered on
a green turf, browsed over by some sheep.'

from 'Edinburgh: Picturesque Notes' by Robert Louis Stevenson 1878

THE SCOTTISH NATIONAL GALLERY OF
MODERN ART · BELFORD ROAD

Scotland's largest collection of modern art is housed in what was formerly
a school. The flag bedecked gallery, set among trees and grass, can be
reached from the centre of the town by following the wooded walkway
which runs from Stockbridge, via the Dean Village, along the banks of the
Water of Leith.

(next page)

HERIOT ROW

INDIA STREET

INDIA STREET

THE NATIONAL GALLERY OF SCOTLAND

DUNDAS STREET

The tall buildings of Dundas Street fall away sharply towards Inverleith.
The uninterrupted view from the top of this street shows clearly the
elevation on which the New Town was constructed.

THE COLONIES · ABBEYHILL

The Colonies, of which there are several in Edinburgh, were built in the
latter half of the nineteenth century by Cooperative Building Societies to
provide houses for working-class owner-occupiers. The simple two-storey
houses were originally sold for about £200 each. In style they have been
compared to a Georgian version of fishermen's cottages.

THE MEADOWS.

To the south of the city lie the Meadows, in an area once covered by the South Loch. For many years this loch provided local brewers with water until it was drained in the eighteenth century and the land reclaimed. Subsequently the Meadows were used as a pleasure ground, and a site for international exhibitions, but their main function has been to provide a tranquil area of greenery where the public can walk and relax.

The details from the outer wall of the house represent: left, Moses reaching out to receive the tablets of the law; and, right, the initials I·M and M·A of James Mosman and his wife Mariot Arres – who built the house and were its first occupants. James Mosman was a wealthy goldsmith and a devoted follower of Mary Stuart.

JOHN KNOX'S HOUSE · HIGH STREET

This house is the oldest dwelling in the city, dating from about 1490. It has been preserved intact mainly because of its association with John Knox who, in fact, only lived here for a few years before his death. The architecture is typical of the time of Mary Queen of Scots.

NEW TOWN DOOR

CHARLOTTE SQUARE

Charlotte Square was one of the last parts of the New Town to be
completed. On summer days the gardens are open and shoppers
and office-workers picnic on the grass.

**LOOKING NORTH-EAST FROM
THE OUTLOOK TOWER**

The clear winter light picks out the dome of the Bank of Scotland on
the Mound. The rooftops recede towards distant snow.

ST. GILES' AND RAMSAY GARDEN
The cat on the roof of Ramsay Garden places a tentative paw over the edge.

THE CASTLE FROM QUEEN'S PARK

JAMES' COURT

One of several examples in the upper part of the Royal Mile of what
imaginative restoration can achieve.

THE SCOTT MONUMENT

Standing two hundred feet high at the east end of Princes Street, the Scott
Monument has become a landmark as famous, in its way, as the Castle or
St. Giles. A white marble statue of Sir Walter Scott sits beneath its arches;
a Border plaid over his shoulder, and his favourite highland stag-hound,
Maida, at his feet. Above him the edifice is decorated with sixty-four
characters from his novels and sixteen statuettes of Scottish poets.

INDEX OF PLACES